the Alleluia Affair

Malcolm Boyd the Alleluia Affair

Word Books, Publisher
Waco, Texas

THE ALLELUIA AFFAIR

Library of Congress catalog card number: 74-27474

Printed in the United States of America.

Scripture quotations are from the Revised
Standard Version of the Bible,
copyright 1946 (renewed 1973), 1956, ——————
and © 1971 by the Division of Christian
Education of the National Council
of the Churches of Christ in the USA, and
are used by permission.

To
Daniel and Elizabeth
Corrigan

1

Jesus pulled his legs free.

The rusty nails that had held his feet captive fell clanking below the cross.

It was not difficult now to free his left hand, then the right one. He slid easily down from the full-size wooden cross in the sanctuary of an inner-city church in Indianapolis.

Next he walked into the adjoining parish hall. He passed by Catherine Coombs of the altar guild, who fainted. Jesus washed in the men's room—he got the blood off his body—and left the building, walking toward the city's hub, Monument Circle.

It was a hot day, so he felt okay in his loincloth.

Jesus had a bit more difficulty disengaging himself from a gold processional cross in an East Side church in Manhattan, yet within just a few moments he was free.

After he had borrowed a soiled vestment to wear, he headed south toward Rockefeller Center.

A cab driver moving along Madison Avenue in the seventies saw Jesus, who was still wearing his crown of thorns. Before he knew what he was doing, the driver had smashed the cab into the plate-glass window of an art gallery.

Moments later when a distinguished actress saw Jesus, she lost her composure.

However, a dog standing on the corner wagged his tail and walked up to Jesus to get acquainted.

In Paris, sixty Jesuses freed from crosses walked toward the *Arc de Triomphe*.

A number wore loincloths and crowns of thorns, while others were attired in the majestic robes of *Christus Rex* and had royal crowns on their heads.

Jesus was visible on the streets of São Paulo, San Francisco, Barcelona, New Delhi, Johannesburg, Sydney, Saigon, Kyoto, Prague, Boston, Stockholm, Peking, and towns and hamlets everywhere.

People came up to talk to Jesus.

If he wore only a loincloth, he was offered a shirt or a coat. If he wore royal robes, others often asked him for a robe to cover their own poverty and need.

Jesus went bareheaded now, without any kind of a crown upon his head. He was offered a haircut, a meal, a place to stay, clothing, help to find a job, or simply companionship as he walked along the street.

The crucified became one of the best-known and most widely discussed matters in the whole world.

"What do you think of when you hear the words 'the crucified'?" a French journalist asked a distinguished professor.

"I think of you and me," replied the professor.

A new sense of compassion was felt by millions of people for the poor, the downtrodden, the hungry or starving, the sick, the prisoners, indeed, the victims of life.

Yet it was feared that this would become a mere passing fancy, a new form of chic, and would not seriously alter the condition of people who were in great need.

Religious leaders throughout the world reacted in press interviews.

Consternation seemed to have taken control of these leaders, for their response was verbose and tended not to be understood by the people.

An Archbishop in England said that "perhaps the church has sinned by over-emphasizing the crucifixion of Jesus Christ while not making relevant the fact of the resurrection to the common man."

A Cardinal in Europe attacked "theological sensationalism" and issued a call for "pastoral control, intellectual discipline, existential soberness, and faithfulness at the foot of the cross."

People ignored the religious leaders, preferring to confront Jesus in the streets and talk to him face-to-face.

On this day in the most powerful nation in all the world, there was the usual number of suicides, serious crimes and sales of hard drugs; more people continued to die in automobile accidents than in foreign wars; and more money was spent for military purposes than for food, housing, and education.

The nation had drive-in restaurants and churches; massage parlors for the living and show-biz burial parlors for the dead; ice cream in a hundred varieties for the kiddies, and unlimited drinks for everybody else.

It had wealth. It had size. It had glamour.

This country had indeed gained the world. Yet a few Cassandras (who were never very popular, in any event) warned that the nation was losing its soul.

2

A couple of years earlier
a very, very rich church—
one that had been built
alongside oil wells and near an
ever sunny ocean—had made a decision.
There must be public signs of faith
for the sake of world-wide evangelism,
it had announced to the press.

The very, very rich church
would make a costly witness to its faith
in Jesus Christ.

The church would rip out its rear wall
and pay great artists
to make a gigantic stained-glass window
to be placed there.
This would be the biggest
and most expensive
stained-glass window in the history
of mankind.
It would be taller than many buildings.
It would show Jesus Christ
on the cross at Golgotha,
crucified between two thieves.

Work on the window
had been pursued vigorously
as if everybody's life
depended upon it.
Great artists
were flown in from everywhere.
Soon it became apparent
that the stained-glass window
would be gorgeous.
The window, as executed,
would be a mélange of rich colors.
The thief nailed to the cross
at the left of Jesus
would be swarthy and deep brown;
the thief nailed to the cross
at the right of Jesus would be jet black.
Jesus himself
would be white as ivory or pearl.

The nails piercing Jesus' body
would be of gold;
the blood of Jesus—
a bit on his hands and feet,
and flowing gently from his side—
would be a rich red;
trees in the background
would be a spring green
such as to make even Vivaldi
exclaim in rapture;
the crosses
were to be a memorable mahogany;
and figures of people milling about
in front of the crosses would be portrayed
in vivid colors
reminiscent of a doge's court.

Jesus' loincloth and crown of thorns
would be of burnt gold,
and the sky the same color,
but with an encroaching turbulence
to be suggested by rich purple
and dark reds.

Today the window was finally completed.
Its cost was astronomical
but understood to be a sacrifice
to the glory of God
and a witness to Jesus Christ.
The amount was paid in full
out of the church's endowments.
Now the dedication ceremony
was being held
on this glorious sunny day.
Bishops were present in droves.
The most important one in the assemblage
blessed the window.

TV cameras turned,
reporters spoke into microphones
and jotted down notes,
and the whole world took notice of the
biggest stained-glass window ever made.
There was even a letter of congratulation
sent by the President
of the most powerful nation
in all the world.
"May God bless you," he wrote.
"And may God continue to bless
the most powerful nation
in all the world."

The church was extraordinarily proud
of its stained-glass window.
It had been written up
in all of the national magazines.
Pictures of the window
were seen by people everywhere.
Already mass pop-culture had been
directly affected by the window.
"Stained Glass" was a new rock hit.
"Love in a Stained-Glass World"
had been announced
as a new high-budgeted film.

There were more serious ramifications
of the stained-glass window
in the socio-political sphere.
"It is not a melting pot that we seek,
but a stained-glass window mosaic,
where everything is together
but maintains its own
peculiar distinctive quality,"
a speaker on race relations had said
a week earlier on national TV.

"We are *all* of us in a moral-ethical
jungle now," a U.S. senator
had said in a recent major speech.
"Yet there can be clean lines
and high purpose
if we will accept the discipline,
the order, and yes, the grandeur
of living in a stained-glass jungle."

Seats at the dedication ceremony
had been reserved long in advance.
Members of the congregation,
a distinguished cross-section
of the prestigious
and the elite, got in.
So did city officials
and an ecumenical sprinkling
of senior clergy representing
main-line churches and synagogues.
Out-of-town guests
were meticulously drawn from the worlds
of politics, religion,
fashion, entertainment,
the military, the arts, and the media.
No one poor was present.
The only blacks
at the ceremony were famous.
"Father, forgive them;
for they know not what they do,"
exclaimed the preacher
who had been flown in from London
for the occasion.

The preacher's sermon
was based on Jesus' seven last words
from the cross.

"Truly, I say to you,
today you will be with me in paradise,"
continued the preacher.

The two thieves
in the stained-glass window
looked at Jesus on the cross.

The wife of an industrial tycoon
started perspiring,
and let her mink stole
slide back on the pew.

"Woman,
behold your son!—Behold your mother,"
said the preacher,
continuing Jesus' last words
from the cross.

Constance Perregrine,
seated in the fourteenth row,
thought of her son
who was next to her in the pew.
Did he understand her long sacrifice
in holding the family together?
Was he grateful that she had postponed
getting the divorce
until the time came for him
to go away to college?

Don Perregrine, seated next to his mother,
looked at the preacher
but did not hear him.
He wondered whether he should enroll
next year at Nebraska U.
or Colorado State.

The sun
streamed through the stained-glass window.
"I thirst," said the preacher,
quoting another of Jesus' last words
on the cross.

So do I, thought the president
of the chamber of commerce.
Yet it was extremely comfortable
inside the building,
for the air conditioning
was operating perfectly.

"My God, my God, why hast thou forsaken me?"
continued the preacher.

I think
the color of Christ's blood in the window
is absolutely too red,
altogether too jarring,
the president of an ad agency said to himself.

It *is* a gorgeous window,
thought a well-known author
who had been commissioned to write a prayer
for the occasion.

The well-known author's prayer,
a copy of which had been inserted
in the printed program that was given
to everybody present at the service, said:
"O Thou Who wast nailed to the cross
and hast borne there the sins of the world,
reach out to us wretched sinners,
lift us up to Thee,
refresh us who thirst,
bestow upon us what Thou dost desire,
nail us to our own crosses,
then take out the nails
at Thine own discretion,
and reward us with the gift of paradise
spent with Thee,
O Crucified One Who dost reign
forever and ever. Amen."

The preacher had a mane of white hair
that grew long down the back of his neck,
around which hung an amethyst cross.
"It is finished," he exclaimed,
quoting from Jesus' words on the cross.

People started to think
of the lavish buffet
that would shortly follow
in the baronial parish hall.
The buffet had been catered by Messolini,
who was a new restaurateur
in the community,
both chic and expensive.

"Father,
into thy hands I commit my spirit,"
the preacher said,
completing the words
of Jesus from the cross.

A frail woman
in the sixth row wept silently.
A fat man in the twenty-third row
tried to wipe away a tear
that had run down
his cheek into his mouth, tasting salty.

I wonder whom we will elect
as the next Bishop,
thought a robed clergyman.

The organ sounded triumphant
in this moment of glory.

The dedication was finished.

People began to fidget in the pews,
women handling their purses,
men folding the printed programs
and placing these in their coat pockets.
Myrtle Epps, who had made ready
the linens and flowers on the altar
for today's event,
gazed at the stained-glass window.
There was no warning before it happened.
When the window seemed to explode
before her very eyes,
she let out a clear scream.

Jesus, the crucified figure in the center
of the vast window,
simply leapt from the cross
and was gone in that same moment.
All that could be seen
in place of the window was blue sky
and jagged fragments of glass.
In the aisles and pews of the church,
hysteria grew around Myrtle Epps.

When all the people had fled the church,
a scroll was found near the altar
that stood below the demolished
stained-glass window.
On the scroll were written these words:

*"When you give a feast, invite the poor,
the maimed, the lame, the blind."*

In the choir loft a second scroll
was shortly discovered
by a member of the choir
who had left behind a small purse,
and came back to retrieve it.

*"Do not lay up for yourselves treasures
on earth, where moth and rust consume
and where thieves break in and steal,
but lay up for yourselves
treasures in heaven,
where neither moth nor rust consumes
and where thieves
do not break in and steal,"*
the scroll announced.

*"For where your treasure is,
there will your heart be also."*

3

Jesus, who had escaped from the stained-glass window, was seen hitch-hiking the next day on Highway 23 not far from the church.

Someone said that he was going to join the migrant farm workers.

The thousands of Jesuses who had come down from crosses and leapt out of church windows all over the world now stayed at YMCA's while they sought temporary employment as laborers.

All the crosses in all of the churches were empty.

Thousands of stained-glass windows were shattered.

"The church preached the resurrection," said an old priest. "Now it is confronted by it."

People were confronted everywhere by Jesus who broke bread in the form of a hamburger bun and drank coffee at counters alongside them. They saw a Jesus who smiled, told a story, and listened to someone else's.

Instead of being nailed to a cross eternally, Jesus did a hard day's work.

He helped to repair a subway, carried trays of dishes, washed floors of office buildings late at night, and cooked meals in steamy kitchens.

Jesus sold tickets in a bus terminal, repaired leaking roofs on houses, collected garbage, and even enrolled for night courses in order to obtain a high school diploma.

It was inside a church in Moscow that an altogether new phenomenon—one that would come to be known by women, men, and children in every corner of the globe—was first observed.

Katerina Palov had been absorbed in her private devotions inside the Moscow church.

Now she looked toward a cross that had once borne Jesus. But to her amazement she saw a body on the cross.

Katerina noticed something very unfamiliar about the body.

When she drew close to the cross, Katerina discovered that a young black man was firmly nailed to the wood.

He did not look like Jesus. He was fully dressed in some kind of a striped uniform.

Investigators discovered that the young black man on the cross was a convict who was serving forty years in a South African prison because he had stolen food from a store in order to feed his starving family.

He did not have a passport. Soviet authorities moved for his immediate extradition.

A handwritten scroll found at the foot of the cross inside the Moscow church contained these words: *"Truly, I say to you, as you did it to one of the least of these, my brethren, you did it to me."*

The scroll continued: *"I was hungry and you gave me no food, I was thirsty and you gave me no drink, I was a stranger and you did not welcome me, naked and you did not clothe me, sick and in prison and you did not visit me."*

It was 3:45 P.M. when Clara Morris stopped off for a moment of prayer in a church on Wilshire Boulevard in Los Angeles.

She was startled to see a body upon a cross, for she was aware that now all crosses were empty.

Drawing close, she saw a brown woman and heard her crying.

The woman was identified as an "Untouchable" who lived in Bombay.

Twelve hours later inside a church in Addis Ababa, a white youth was found nailed to an altar cross that had previously borne Jesus.

The youth told the Ethiopian Red Cross that he lived in Evanston, Illinois. His parents beat him very badly when they had had too much to drink.

There were scars of beatings on his body and his left eye was swollen shut.

So, people began to see that they crucified one another.

Could they stop visiting agonies and terrors upon each other's lives? It dawned upon them that when they placed Jesus on the cross, they also placed one another on it.

Could they let the cross be empty?

Hubert Lacey stopped inside a church near Fleet Street in London.

He wanted to say a prayer for his wife who was dying of cancer. Lacey had only a few moments to spare from his job. Indeed, he was out on assignment to interview a Hollywood actress for the newspaper where he worked as a reporter.

But a cross inside the church held a body.

It was that of a young woman from Dallas who was pregnant.

Lacey learned from Susan, the young woman, that her family had angrily kicked her out when they found that she was going to have a baby although she was unmarried.

They told Susan that her condition deeply offended their religious belief, and they felt that she was damned and therefore no more a member of their family whom they could love.

The reporter picked up a scroll near the cross and read its words: *"Judge not, that you be not judged. For with the judgment you pronounce you will be judged, and the measure you give will be the measure you get."*

Another scroll that the police later found at the foot of the altar in the church said: *"Or what man of you, if his son asks for a loaf, will give him a stone? Or if he asks for a fish, will give him a serpent? If you then, who are evil, know how to give good gifts to your children, how much more will your Father who is in heaven give good things to those who ask him? So whatever you wish that men would do to you, do so to them; for this is the law and the prophets."*

Nancy Fitzhugh had decided when she got up this morning to spend an hour or so alone inside one of her favorite places, the Museum of Art.

Now she was walking slowly through the gallery, absorbed in her thoughts.

She would go up to the third floor and visit one of her most prized exhibits. It was a medieval processional cross designed in tempera and gold on wood. The Italian artist had lived in the fifteenth century.

Once Jesus had been crucified on the cross, his arms stretched out upon the wood, his hands nailed down. Of course, Jesus had recently left the cross, so Nancy would miss seeing him, but she would still have a feeling of spiritual uplift from looking at the old cross itself.

She climbed the stairs to the gallery on the third floor of the art museum.

Nancy walked into the gallery and found the glass case.

The cross was not empty.

A woman dressed in furs and wearing jewels was on the cross.

She was drunk.

Investigators discovered that the woman was married to one of the richest and most famous men in the city.

He had given his wife all the money that she could desire, jewels, homes, servants, cars, and a yacht.

But he could never spare her his valuable time.

His wife had felt desperately alone in the midst of people who were paid to keep her company. Love was a mystery to her.

In the glass case a scroll was found and it said: *"No one can serve two masters: for either he will hate the one and love the other, or he will be devoted to the one and despise the other. You cannot serve God and mammon."*

When Manuel Gonzalez walked inside a small rural Mexican church, he sought a priest.

He found Joe English on the big wooden cross that had once held Jesus.

Joe lived in Cleveland, worked as an insurance salesman, supported his wife and five children, and told the Mexican authorities that he had lost the meaning of life. All that he did was work, pay higher prices and taxes, and grow increasingly isolated from his family. He could not communicate with his wife and children.

Lately he had come to hate his job but he knew no other way to earn a living. He was behind in payments. He spent two full hours each day on a noisy and smelly highway driving to and from his office.

Joe went to church for the sake of his family, but he no longer believed in anything. He drank and ate too much. Joe asked for psychiatric help when they got his body down from the cross.

A scroll found underneath Joe's cross contained these words: *"Consider the lilies of the field, how they grow; they neither toil nor spin; yet I tell you, even Solomon in all his glory was not arrayed like one of these. But if God so clothes the grass of the field, which today is alive and tomorrow is thrown into the oven, will he not much more clothe you, o men of little faith?"*

It continued: *"Therefore do not be anxious, saying, 'What shall we eat?' or 'What shall we drink?' or 'What shall we wear?' For the Gentiles seek all these things; and your heavenly Father knows that you need them all. But seek first his kingdom and his righteousness, and all these things shall be yours as well."*

Later the priest found another scroll next to the altar.

It read: *"Blessed are the poor in spirit, for theirs is the kingdom of heaven."*

Inside a jail in a country that had been seized by a military regime, a political prisoner was subjected once again to torture.

He cried out helplessly, struggling to endure excruciating pain.

His torturers were all loyal members of the church.

A cross hung on the wall of the room in which he was tortured.

A military chaplain knew that the prisoner was the victim of men who acted under orders, for the chaplain served the same command.

Afterward the prisoner lay on the floor of his cell. He felt that he could bear no more of such savage pain. He fainted.

His torturers were now inside the room where the man had suffered his agony.

One of them glanced at the cross and he screamed in panic. The others recoiled in terror from what they saw.

The prisoner whom they had tortured hung upon the cross.

A scroll beneath the cross said: *"Blessed are the merciful, for they shall obtain mercy."*

Brenda Hayes drove to a suburban church for a benefit society luncheon that would be followed by a fashion show. She would meet most of her friends there.

Walking toward the parish house where the luncheon would be served, she looked inside the church. Then Brenda noticed a hole in a stained-glass window which had held Jesus on the cross. Jesus was gone.

A tiny figure hung on a cross in the jagged, half-empty space. She was an emaciated, starving child.

Near the stained-glass window Brenda saw a scroll. It contained these words: *"Blessed are you poor, for yours is the kingdom of God. Blessed are you that hunger now, for you shall be satisfied. Blessed are you that weep now, for you shall laugh."*

In Toronto, Kate Longmans dropped into a church to light a candle and say a prayer.

She found Jacob Reuben, who lived in Chicago, on the cross. He told her that he was a practicing Jew, and had been harassed and persecuted because of his faith. Christians crucified him because he was a Jew.

A scroll found near Jacob Reuben's cross contained these words: *"Who are my mother and my brothers?—Here are my mother and my brothers! Whoever does the will of God is my brother, and sister, and mother."*

The college chapel was empty when Brian Dobbs entered quietly.

He took a seat in one of the pews on the left side of the chapel. It was finals week, and this place would afford him privacy and a peaceful opportunity to study for his next day's exam.

But he was startled to hear someone softly crying.

Then he saw a figure hanging on the distant cross that stood upon the altar.

Brian drew close to the cross.

Eugene Moore hung on it. He explained that he was seventy-six years old. His three children were married and had families of their own, so they had no place for him.

Now he lived alone in a rotting hotel in a crime-ridden downtown section of Detroit. The elderly and sick people who occupied the rooms of the hotel were often mugged and robbed during the days, and were afraid to walk on the streets at night.

Eugene Moore did not have enough money to eat properly.

He had been rejected and felt very, very tired and without hope.

A scroll that lay on the college chapel altar contained these handwritten words: *"Foxes have holes, and birds of the air have nests; but the Son of man has nowhere to lay his head."*

Certain crucifixions were more mysterious than others.

Nurse Veronique de Saussune began her day at the Paris hospital by dropping into the chapel to meditate for a few moments.

When she pushed open the chapel door, immediately she saw a man upon the altar cross.

Tubes ran into his nostrils, arms, and legs.

He was from Rome and was dying of cancer.

The pain caused by his illness showed itself in the agony marked on his face.

The man on the cross told Nurse Veronique de Saussune that his suffering was redeemed and given meaning because Jesus had already suffered and died on the cross for him.

A scroll found in the hospital chapel read: *"Enter by the narrow gate; for the gate is wide and the way is easy, that leads to destruction, and those who enter it are many. For the gate is narrow and the way is hard, that leads to life, and those who find it are few."*

4

People wanted very earnestly
to stop crucifying each other.
They honestly preferred loving to hating,
life instead of death,
and clearly perceived the harm
that they had brought to others as well as
to themselves.
It occurred to them
that they had apparently
paid lip-service to Christianity
without taking it very seriously
or even considering the possibility
of actually practicing it.
They saw how they had used
the cross as a symbol
in their churches' stained-glass windows
and on their altars, yet had not delved
at all deeply into its real meanings.
They had wanted to find out
what the crucifixion
of Jesus Christ really meant.

Now they wanted to know
what the resurrection
of Jesus Christ really meant.
Jesus' seven last words from the cross
were universally examined.
"Father, forgive them;
for they know not what they do."

It was understood by an ever-increasing
number of people that sin
was not something
to be superficially equated
with sexuality,
as they had previously been taught.
More and more people were able to see
that the greatest sin
was probably an exaggerated form
of self-preoccupation
that simply shut out God
and everybody else.
The question was raised:
Could the very unawareness of such sin
be the gravest sin?

"Truly, I say to you,
Today you will be with me in paradise."

Acceptance now came to be offered
more freely to others.
For everybody
had to confront the question:
Who is worthy?
Who is unworthy?
Scrolls were found in subways,
bus terminals,
and supermarkets that contained
only these words:
"Love your enemies."

A deeper human relationship
came to be affirmed.
"Woman,
behold your son!—Behold your mother!"

People felt
a deeper belonging to one another.
Love came to be comprehended
as a responsibility, even a commandment,
and not just something
to make one feel better.

"I thirst."

Need was no longer perceived so selfishly
as it had been before.
Universal need was seen more clearly
in its many ramifications.
People asked:
"Who is my brother or sister?"
"Who is my neighbor?"

"My God, my God,
why hast thou forsaken me?"

People who had fallen into a sense of
being utterly abandoned
now gave voice to their feelings
and awareness of existence itself.
They cried to God:
for justice, for explanation.
They cried to other people for
sharing and love:
Brother, sister, where are you?

"It is finished."

A new sense of accomplishment and pride
came to the elderly and others
who had done their best,
run their course faithfully,
completed a hard but necessary task,
or stuck with a problem
that required infinite patience.
Countless people gained a new respect
for others as well as themselves.
In fact, they recognized Jesus
in members of their families, friends,
acquaintances, and strangers.
Too, they recognized Jesus in themselves
and so ceased to hate themselves
and be swallowed-up in guilt and despair.

Jesus' last words from the cross,
'Father,
into thy hands I commit my spirit,"
now provided a tremendous reassurance
to countless people.

This was seen as an affirmation of faith
in which they could share.
Soon people began to see that they
could make Jesus' resurrection a reality
in their own lives and those of others.
So, crucifixion and resurrection
were not abstractions
or events buried in the past.

Crucifixion happened now.

Resurrection happened now.

5

It was an excellent time in the lives of a great many people.

Faith came to be actually practiced more and more in everyday life.

Hope was genuine, rooted in an understanding of the resurrection.

Love abounded, as crucifixions became few and far between.

But now evil struck with relentless terror.

A sudden war left cities in waste, many thousands of lives destroyed, homes leveled, and unspeakable brutality practiced on the living.

A wave of persecution, imprisonment, torture, and utter regimentation of life swept the world. There was horror in the skies and on the earth.

Many could scarcely remember when there had been hope, beauty, and love.

An official pronouncement said that all expressions of faith must be rooted out without delay.

The state wanted pragmatism to exist in the place of mystery, grinding obedience where there had once been freedom of the spirit.

Faith? No place was allowed for it in the superstate. Indeed, faith, hope, and love were seen as subversive. People were now required to base their existence only on total submission to authority, disciplined action in the present, and the proper performance of prescribed roles.

All faiths represented in the society were punished.

Followers of Jesus, however, were attacked with the utmost violence. This was because of Jesus' deep involvement in human life, culminating in his crucifixion and resurrection.

Jesus' action established the primacy of the Kingdom of God over the state, and offered eternal hope.

So, the memory of Jesus was to be eradicated from everyone's consciousness. It was commanded that all crosses should be destroyed.

Crosses were smashed, chopped up, thrown upon bonfires that also consumed Bibles, or melted in furnaces.

A few crosses were saved and hidden, but at the cost of terrible risk for the people who were involved.

The very idea of God as Lover, entering into human life and dying for the sake of people's salvation, then being resurrected from the dead and representing the Kingdom of God as an eternal homeland which had even greater power than the state, was anathema.

A scroll found in a public place said: *"In the world you have tribulation; but be of good cheer, I have overcome the world."*

Followers of Jesus were publicly placed on trial, privately tortured.

But their faith persisted and grew stronger.

Earlier when the Jesuses had come down from all the crosses, and entered into the resurrection stream of life, they had set in motion a new force that could not be resisted by all the powers available to the state authorities.

For millions of people had learned how to see the reality of Jesus' presence in one another's lives.

Crosses were drawn with pencils on state posters that were publicly exhibited.

Chalk marks in the form of crosses were everywhere on pavements and walls of buildings.

"Emmanuel, God with us" was painted in red on a public utility building.

Scrolls were found. They said *"Love your enemies."* And also, *"Lo, I am with you always."*

People walking along the streets sometimes whispered to others, friends and strangers alike, "Hello, Jesus."

The idea of Jesus as a thirty-year-old man who had long hair and wore a long robe was no longer a part of people's consciousness.

For, of course, they saw Jesus in one another.

A stranger on a street passed a stout, white, middle-aged man wearing a double-breasted business suit and carrying a briefcase, and said "Hello, Jesus."

A janitor walked past the desk of a black woman who was the manager of an office and said "Hello, Jesus."

A lonely, solitary woman who had worked for thirty years in a building where no one had ever been her friend now found herself surrounded by friends.

An elderly man who had once been a religious leader, and suffered from spiritual pride although he looked humble, was quietly helped by new friends to free himself from the old shackles and be a new person in Jesus.

People shared food and clothing, conversation and books, transportation and hope.

More scrolls were found in public places.

"*Truly, truly, I say to you, unless a grain of wheat falls into the earth and dies, it remains alone; but if it dies, it bears much fruit,*" said one.

Another scroll read: "*I am the resurrection and the life; he who believes in me, though he die, yet shall he live, and whoever lives and believes in me shall never die.*"

Small groups gathered together for worship and meditation in rooms and apartments.

They took turns reading Scripture aloud to each other, prayed from their own hearts, hummed or very, very quietly sang beloved old hymns that were forbidden. They swung an incense pot if they liked, sometimes even went so far as to place lighted candles on a table or a mantel.

If one such group was arrested, a dozen new ones sprung up.

The followers of Jesus were listed as subversives because their ultimate allegiance was to the Kingdom of God and its tenets of belief rather than to the authoritarian state.

Enraged and baffled, authorities of the state announced that a public execution would take place in the great square at the center of the capital city.

A twenty-three-year-old follower of Jesus would be crucified.

While the authorities knew that they were conjuring up images highly dangerous to the state by utilizing the cross for this execution, their anger overrode wiser counsel.

On the announced day of the execution, ten thousand people crowded into the city square.

Thousands more filled the nearby streets.

The authorities brought in their victim and prepared to place her on the cross.

"Crucify us!" the cry started from the crowd.

Within moments ten thousand people shouted in unison.

"Crucify us!" "Crucify us!"

Thousands more in the streets echoed their cry.

Soldiers now turned their guns upon the people.

"Crucify us!" the thousands chanted.

"Crucify us!"

"Crucify us!"

Some of the soldiers now wept openly. They began to throw their weapons on the ground.

Other soldiers embraced people in the chanting crowd.

The power of the state was broken.

A new order had come into being.

6

Everywhere people who had stopped trying to make needed changes in life, strive for God's justice on earth, and discern beauty before their eyes, decided to try once more.

And people who had never really given up, but often felt discouraged or even despairing, decided that they would try harder.

They would try harder to embrace faith, letting it open up closed rooms and ghettos of their lives.

They would try harder to nurture hope, letting it combat an ever-encroaching malaise of cynicism that threatened life.

They would try harder to accept and give love.

A scroll was found in a public place.
Its handwritten message read:

PHOTO CREDITS—in order of appearance

PART 1

Image/Leo M. Johnson
Image/Jack Corn
Ed Wallowitch
Ed Wallowitch

PART 2

Camera One/Dale Dougherty

PART 3

Image/Bryan Moss
Image/Richard T. Lee
Ed Wallowitch
Ed Wallowitch
Image/Brian Holtsclaw
Ed Wallowitch
Image/Jack Corn

PART 4

Ed Wallowitch
Ed Wallowitch
Ed Wallowitch
Ed Wallowitch
Image/Randy West
Ed Wallowitch
Ed Wallowitch
Ed Wallowitch

PART 5

Image/Ira Rosenberg
Ed Wallowitch
Ed Wallowitch
Ed Wallowitch
Ed Wallowitch
Ed Wallowitch
Ed Wallowitch
Image/Randy Singer

PART 6

Sean Rice/Sculptor

230

Boyd, Malcolm
    The Alleluia Affair

DATE DUE			
2/10/76			
Dec 5			
OCT 2 4 1977			